I'm Reading About

IDAHO

The Gem State!

GALLOPADE

by Carole Marsh

Printed and Manufactured in Peachtree City, GA., USA
www.gallopade.com

Book design: John Hanson

Editorial manager: Janice Baker

Current Edition ©September 2024

Idaho is a great state.

It is one of a kind.

What makes Idaho special?

Let's read about it

and see!

NATIVE AMERICANS

Who lived in Idaho first?

Native Americans did!

They moved around to find food.
They hunted for animals to eat.
They fished in Idaho's rivers.
They gathered fruits and seeds and nuts.

EXPLORERS

Meriwether Lewis and William Clark came to Idaho in 1805. They were sent to explore new territory.

They traveled along Idaho's rivers and through Idaho's mountains. Lewis and Clark learned about Idaho's plants and animals.

SETTLEMENT

A group of Mormons traveled westward across America.
They started the first settlement in Idaho in 1860.
They named it Franklin.

Soon after Franklin was founded, gold was discovered in Idaho.
People rushed to Idaho to look for gold!

Franklin

STATEHOOD

Idaho was the 43rd state
to join the United States of America!

Isn't it great,
to be a state!
I bet Idaho
could hardly wait!

Idaho became a state in 1890.

Idaho

The 43rd State

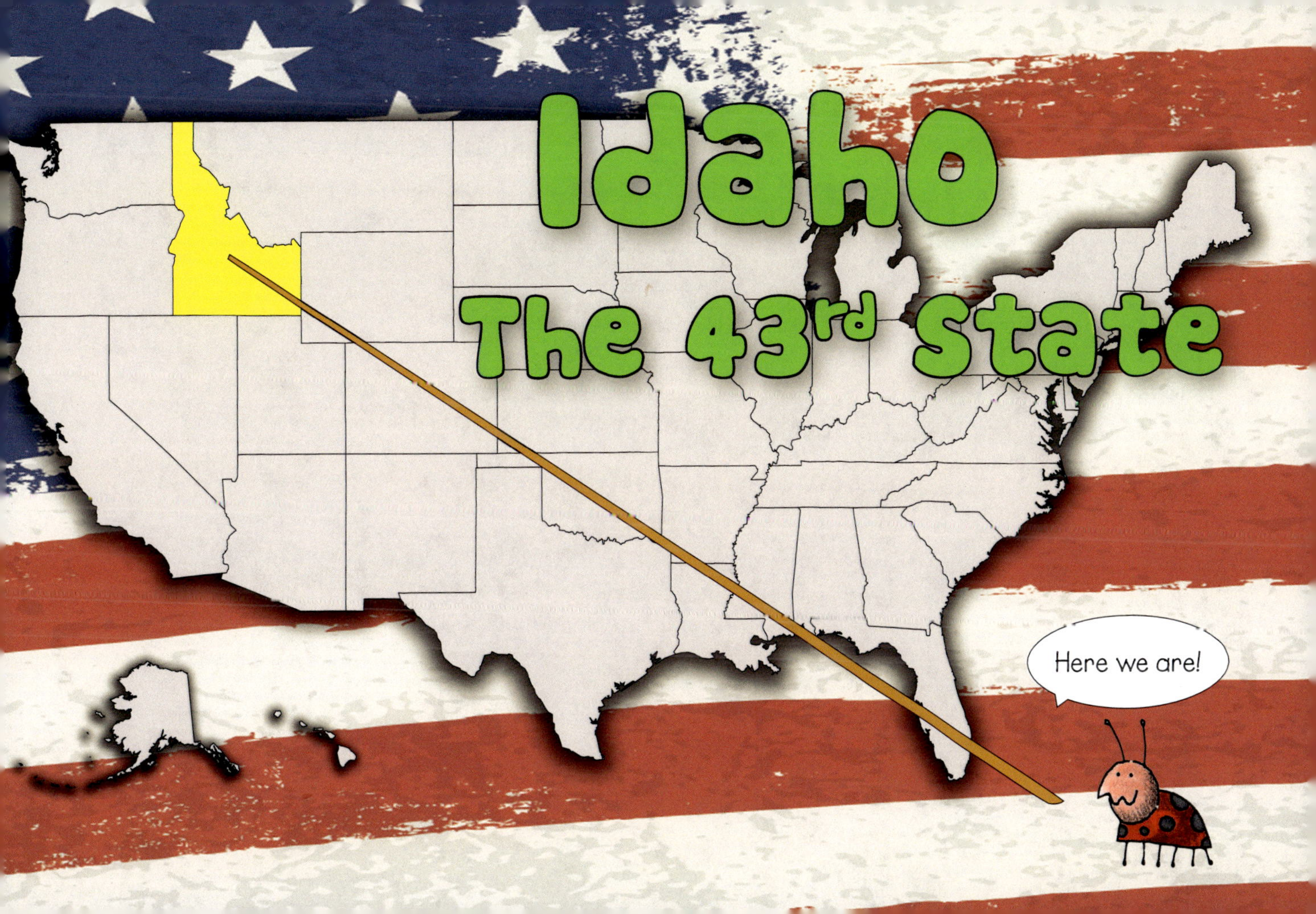

FLAG

I am the state flag.

What color am I?
I am blue.

Look at me.
What else do you see?

I fly high over the state of Idaho!

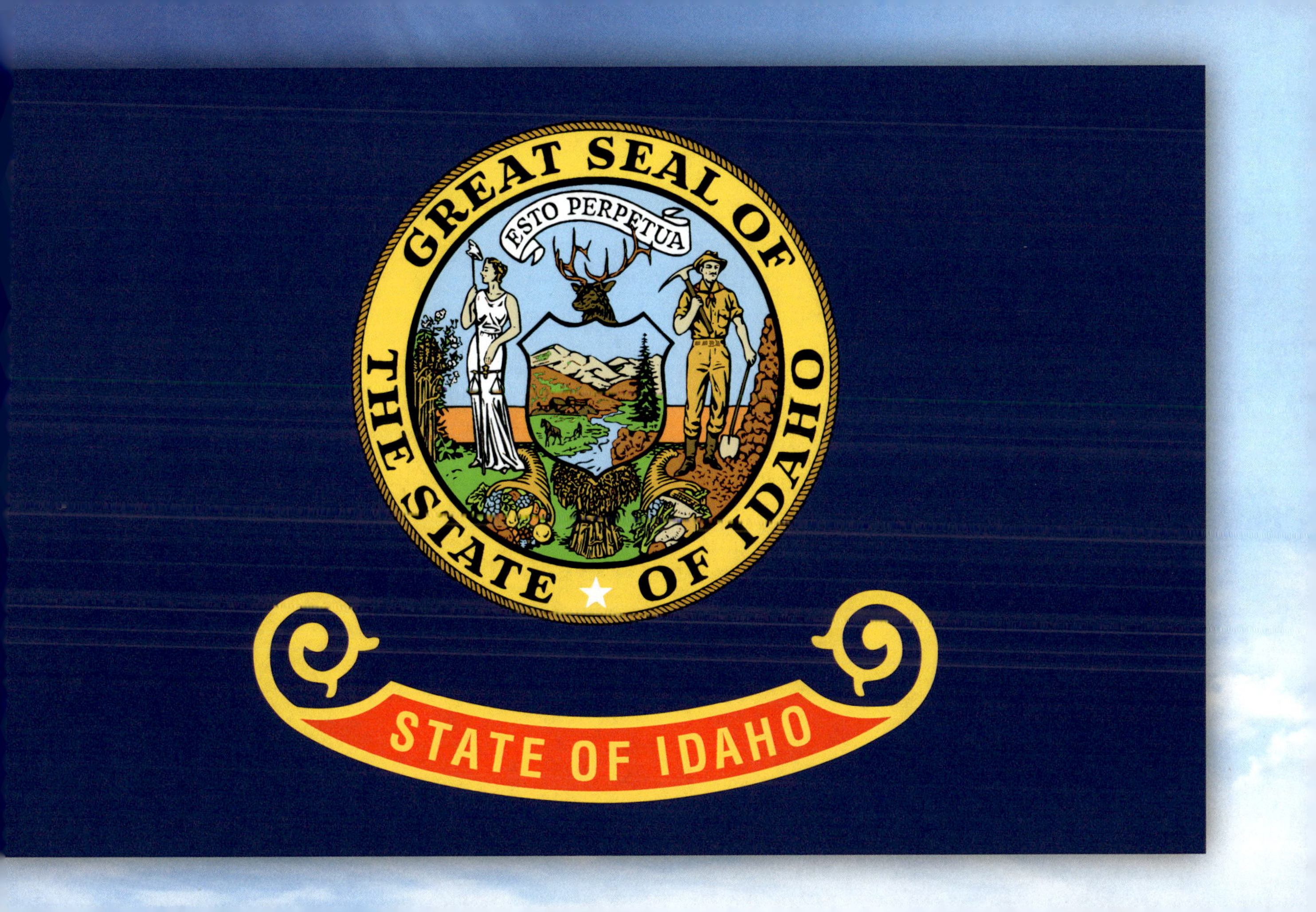
GREAT SEAL OF THE STATE OF IDAHO
ESTO PERPETUA
STATE OF IDAHO

CAPITAL

Say hello to Boise,
the capital city of Idaho!

There is an important building in Boise.
It is the State Capitol.
Idaho's laws are made there!

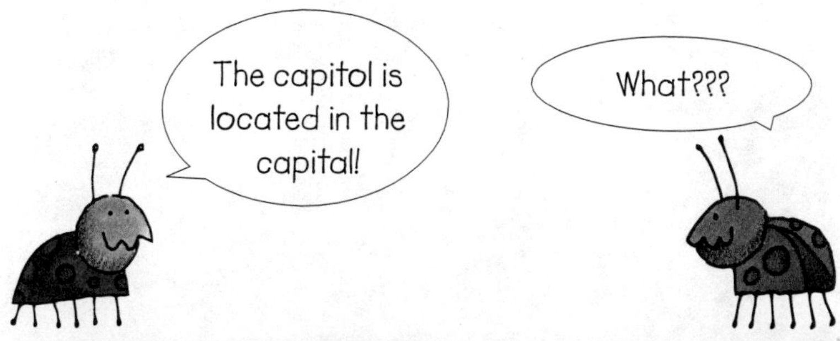

Capitol

Capital

SEAL

I am a seal,
but I am not the State Seal.
If I were, I would be very important.
I would be stamped on many official papers.
(Ouch, that might hurt!)

GREAT SEAL OF THE STATE OF IDAHO
ESTO PERPETUA

Now, that's official!

NICKNAME

State nicknames are fun!
State nicknames are great!
They share fun facts
about each state!

Idaho's nickname is "The Gem State."

Many types of beautiful gems have been found in Idaho!

The Gem State
IDAHO
0004NE
THE GEM STATE
2011
0004NE
03
My nickname is "The Red Bug."

BORDERS

Look at Idaho.
Idaho is in a region called "the Northwest."

Idaho borders six other states. It also borders the country of Canada.
Find Idaho and its neighbors on the map!

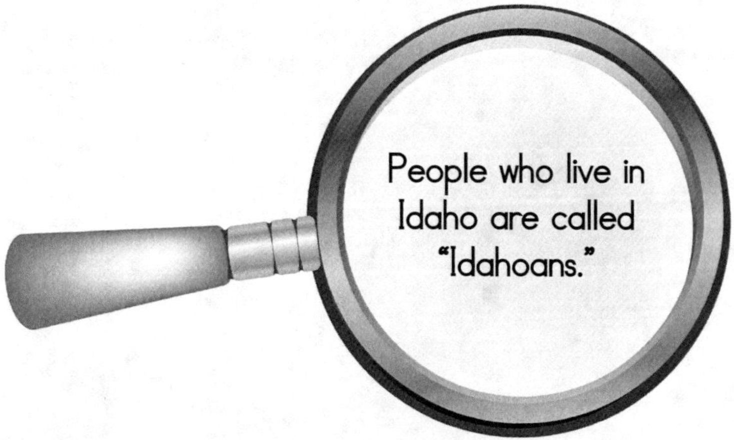

Borders

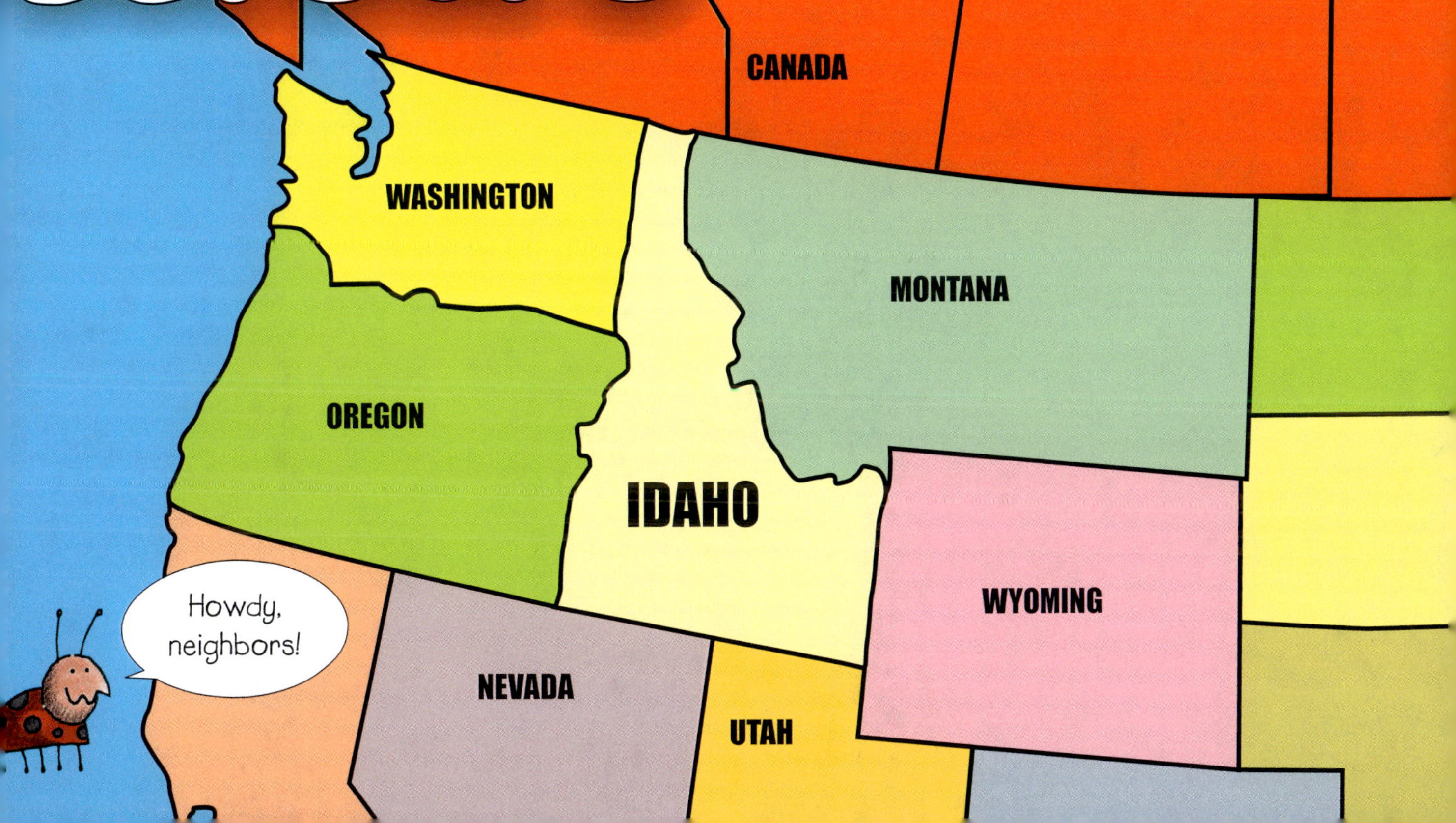
CANADA
WASHINGTON
MONTANA
OREGON
IDAHO
WYOMING
NEVADA
UTAH
Howdy, neighbors!

COUNTIES

Idaho is divided into 44 counties.
Counties are a form of local government.
Counties provide services that people need!
Those services include:

Schools **Parks** **Libraries** **Police**
Firefighters **and More!**

Counties

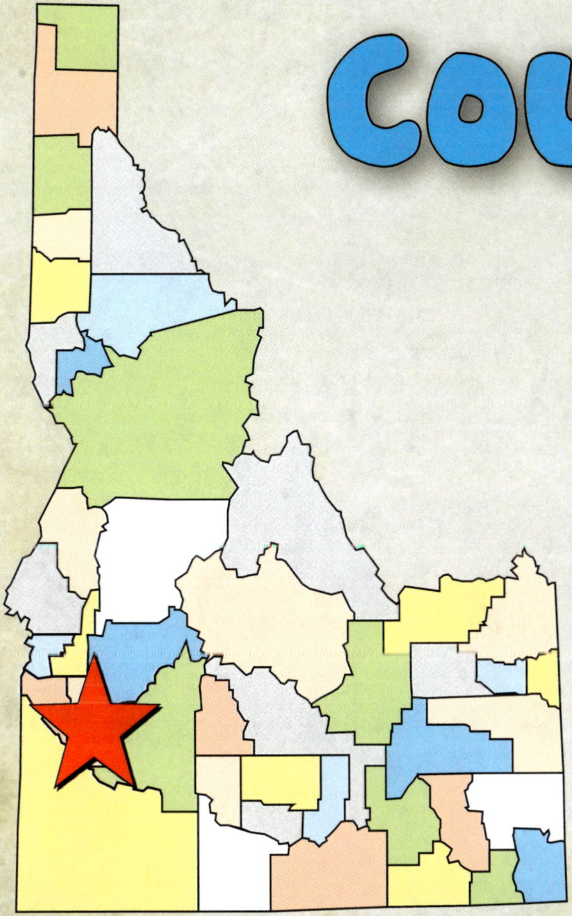

IDAHO'S CAPITAL, BOISE, IS IN ADA COUNTY.

PEOPLE

Many famous peopl

Sacagawea

Helped guide the Lewis and Clark Expedition

Gutzon Borglum

Created the sculpture of four U.S. presidents on Mount Rushmore

Ernest Hemingway

Author of many novels includi The Old Man and the Sea

call our state home!

Joe Albertson
Founder of Albertsons grocery stores

J.R. Simplot
Founder of the J.R. Simplot Company known as the "French Fry King"

Picabo Street
Won Olympic gold medal in alpine skiing event

Mountain Bluebird

I am the state bird, and I fly
over Idaho, proud and high.

As I fly, up in the sky,
I flap my wings to tell you "Hi!"

The Idaho state bird is the Mountain Bluebird.

BIRD

Syringa

FLOWER

I am the Syringa.
I am the state flower.

I grow where it's warm and sunny.
I bloom in spring and summer.
I help make Idaho beautiful!

Look at me! Smell me!
Native American used my
branches to make bows
and arrows!

Western White Pine

I am a Western White Pine—I'm the state tree.
Northern Idaho is where to find me.

My roots run deep, they keep me strong.
My leaves stay green, all year long.

I stand up straight, big and tall.
Don't climb too high—it would hurt to fall!

TREE

Monarch Butterfly

I am the Monarch Butterfly.
I am the state insect.

I flit and I fly from flower to flower.
I am looking for nectar to drink.

Look at my beautiful wings.
What colors do you see?

INSECT

Lakes

Let's go to the lake!

We can wade in the water.
We can ride on a boat.

We can jump off the dock
onto an inner tube float!

Idaho's lakes are home to many animals:

Fish **Snakes** **Birds** **Turtles** **Salamanders** **and More!**

LAKES

Rocky Mountains

MOUNTAINS

Idaho's Rocky Mountains are the place to be.
Hiking, fishing, camping—
fun for you and me.

Winter weather brings lots of snow.
Temperatures drop to freezing and below!

Rivers

RIVERS

Idaho has many rivers.
People like to use rivers for boating and fishing!

This habitat is home to many animals:

Birds Deer Snakes Frogs Fish and More!

The Snake River is the longest river in Idaho.

Shoshone Falls

LANDMARK

Shoshone Falls is a beautiful waterfall.
It is located on the Snake River in southern Idaho.
The waterfall is 212 feet tall.
Shoshone Falls is often called the
"Niagara of the West."

It is best to visit Shoshone Falls in
the spring and summer.
Melted snow adds more water to
the waterfall!

Idaho Crops

Potatoes

Hay

Wheat

Sugarbeets

Potatoes are my personal favorite!

AGRICULTURE

Idaho has many farms.
Why?
Because Idaho has good soil and a mild climate!

Some of Idaho's top crops are:

Potatoes **Hay** **Wheat** **Sugarbeets**

Hey!
Don't forget about me!
I am an Idaho cow.
I produce lots of milk
to make dairy products!

Sports in Idaho

SPORTS

Baseball! Basketball! Football!
Idaho has it all.

Whether you like to watch or play,
You are sure to have a ball!

Broncos **Bengals** **Vandals**

& More!

Idaho: Home of the Potato

CLAIM TO FAME

You can't think about Idaho without thinking about potatoes!

Idaho grows more potatoes than any other state. Potatoes love Idaho's soil and mild weather. There is even a potato called the "Idaho potato."

Potatoes are full of important vitamins and minerals!

GLOSSARY

climate: weather conditions in an area over a long period of time

expedition: a journey to explore or research something

gem: a beautiful stone that has been cut and polished

habitat: a place where plants or animals naturally live

laws: rules made by the government

nectar: a sugary fluid made by plants

region: an area that has similar characteristics

sculpture: a carving in stone or wood

settlement: the first community in an area

territory: an area of land that is ruled by another state or country